IMPRESSIONS of

WALES

I BN

1 1 0563622 1

Produced by AA Publishing
© AA Media Limited 2006

Published by AA Publishing (a trading name of AA Media Limited, whose registered
office is Fanum House, Basing View, Basingstoke, Hampshire RG21 4EA;
registered number 06112600)
Reprinted July 2009

ISBN-10: 0 7495 4862 2
ISBN-13: 978 0 7495 4862 9
A04179

Printed by C&C Offset Printing, China

Front cover: Conwy Castle and Telford's Suspension Bridge.

IMPRESSIONS of
WALES

Picture Acknowledgements

All photographs are held in the Automobile Association's own photo library (AA World Travel Library) and were taken by the following photographers:

M Allwood-Coppin 49; Pat Aithie 27, 42, 58, 67; Jeff Beazley 11; Ian Burgum 8, 15, 22, 30, 31, 32, 35, 40, 41, 51, 52, 56, 57, 65, 66, 68, 69, 70, 76, 77, 78, 79, 81, 90, 95; Derek Croucher 45, 53, 86; Alan Grierley 10, 29; Anthony Hopkins 63; Richard Ireland 72, 80; Nick Jenkins 3, 5, 14, 18, 23, 28, 38, 38, 54, 59, 60, 61, 71, 84, 85; Caroline Jones 9, 12, 37, 47, 48, 55, 73, 75, 83, 88, 94; Graham Matthews 16, 19, 25, 36, 43, 62, 93; Andrew Molyneux 50; Colin Molyneux 46, 92; Colin & Andrew Molyneux 17, 20; Rich Newton 26, 33, 64, 87; Wyn Voysey 13, 21, 34; Harry Williams 82, 91, 74.

Opposite: the Millennium Stadium at Cardiff.

INTRODUCTION

Of all the regions of Britain, the western outpost of Wales has always maintained its historical independence and individuality – despite becoming part of the Union as long ago as 1536. It is a spirit communicated through the nationalism of its people, and in the defence and promotion of its Celtic mother-tongue. Wales boasts the longest placename in Britain, and its tongue-twisting names baffle the uninitiated who seek in vain for the vowels.

Impressions of Wales captures the Welsh spirit as it is reflected in landscape, which varies from the sheer waterfalls and craggy mountains of the north, through deserted hill country and along the lovely, sweeping coasts of Ceredigion and Pembrokeshire down to the busy, urban south.

Medieval English sailors crossing the Irish Sea first gave Snowdonia its name – this wild, northern, rocky region always seemed to be brushed with snow. To the Welsh, though, it was known as Eyri, the 'abode of eagles', and in 1951, 827 square miles (2,142sq km) of Snowdonia were designated as one of the first and largest of Britain's national parks. The westward-pointing finger of the Lleyn Peninsula has some of the best beaches in North Wales, while the resorts of the north coast around Llandudno show an altogether gentler aspect.

The Welsh coastline is the first part of Britain to receive the balmy influence of the Gulf Stream, and at times the effect can seem positively Mediterranean – a scene accentuated in the bizarre village of Portmeirion, with its rescued Italianate buildings. The rocky points of the glorious Pembrokeshire Coast stretch out into the blue waters of the Irish Sea, haunted by seabirds, and its cliff-hemmed sandy bays are perfect for water-sports. The gorse-studded peninsula of the Gower, with its quiet beaches, coves and charming fishing villages, has long been the playground of the industrial cities of South Wales.

Inland, the Beacons range, which rise above the lush valley of the River Usk, have their own national park. These sandstone mountains stand like a petrified wave about to break over the ancient town of Brecon. West lies the wild expanse of the Fforest Fawr and the Black Mountain, while to the east on the border with England are the Black Mountains. South of here, the industrial valleys of South Wales, green with the shoots of regeneration, reach up from Glamorgan's largely undiscovered Heritage Coast, and the great city of Cardiff. The Welsh capital since 1955, Cardiff is the natural focal point of the coastal plain, and the southern gateway to this very special land ever since the Romans and Normans built their fortifications at places such as Caerleon, Cardiff, Monmouth and Raglan.

Mid Wales is the least-known part of the country, yet it contains the source of the mighty Severn and the Wye; the Welsh 'Lake District', comprising the huge complex of reservoirs of the Vyrnwy, Elan and Clywedog Valleys; and some of the finest stretches of unspoilt coastline, along Cardigan Bay. You can walk, ride or cycle here and not see another soul.

Opposite: sunrise over Swansea's working docks.

The Swallow Falls near Betws-y-Coed in Snowdonia National Park.
Opposite: Caerphilly Castle, in Mid Glamorgan, dates from the 13th century. It was restored in
1958 after centuries of neglect.

Neolithic Lliwy burial chamber, Moelfre, Anglesey.

The five peaks of the Cader Idris massif loom to the south of Lake Gwernan in Snowdonia National Park.

Llandudno, at the eastern side of Conwy Bay. The pier marks the eastern end of the Victorian seaside town's `2-mile (1-km) promenade. Its pavilion was destroyed by fire in 1994.

Tall-y-Llyn in the steep-sided Dysini Valley, between Dolgellau and Machynlleth.

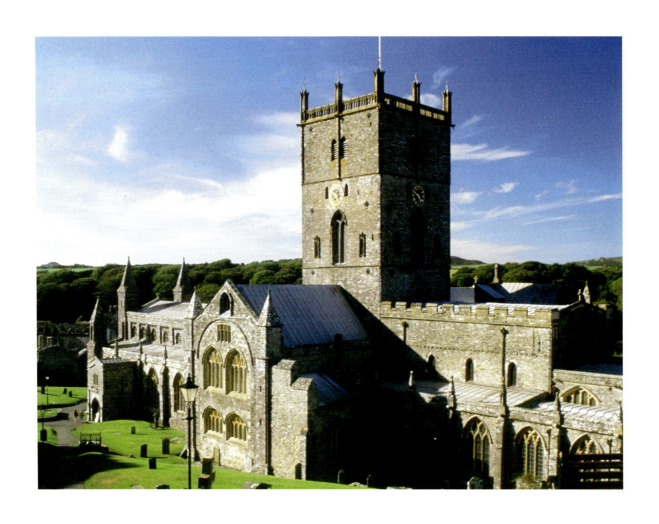

St David's Cathedral, in Dyfed, was founded by the patron saint of Wales in the 1st century.
Opposite: the beach at Mewslade Bay beneath the limestone cliffs of the Gower Heritage Coast,
in West Glamorgan.

The north coast of the Lleyn Peninsula, near the village of Morfa Nefyn.

*Opposite: Llyn Brianne, a reservoir for Swansea in the Upper Tywi Valley. It was built between 1968 and 1972
with a 300-ft (91-m) dam.*

The harbour at Aberystwyth, a lively seaside resort and university town on Cardigan Bay, Dyfed.

Llanbedrog, one of the resorts along the southern coast of the Lleyn Peninsula.

The River Usk with the Black Mountains beyond, in the Brecon Beacons National Park.

Harlech Castle looks out over Cardigan Bay, in Gwynedd. Edward I built it as part of his Iron Ring –
the string of fortresses round the coast of North Wales.

A natural promontory at Tenby, in Dyfed, separates the South Beach (above) from the North Beach.

A seal pup on the pebble cove of Martin's Haven, on the Pembrokeshire Coast. Boat rides to Skomer Island depart from here.

Llyn Idwal, in Snowdonia. The cliffs behind are split by the 'chimney' known as the Devil's Kitchen.

Abersoch, a former fishing village at the mouth of the River Soch, on the heel of the Lleyn Peninsula,
is now a burgeoning yachting centre.

The ruins of Dolbadarn Castle, near Llanberis in Gwynedd. Llywelyn the Great built the fortress in the 12th and 13th centuries.
Opposite: on the shore at Penmaenmawr, which looks across Conwy Bay.

Looking north to the summit of Snowdon from Bethania, in the Gwyant Valley.

A roofless 12th-century church, Hen Capel Lligwy, Anglesey.

Two mountain streams, the Glaslyn (above) and the Colwyn, converge near Beddgelert, in Gwynedd.
Opposite: undeveloped coast at Dinas Dinlle, site of an old fort on the Lleyn Peninsula.

Cefn Cyff ridge with the Black Mountains in the distance, Powys.

Hillsides strewn with slate debris form the backdrop to Blaenau Ffestiniog, in Gwynedd.

The Mawddach River estuary at Barmouth, Gwynedd, crossed by the Cambrian coast railway line.

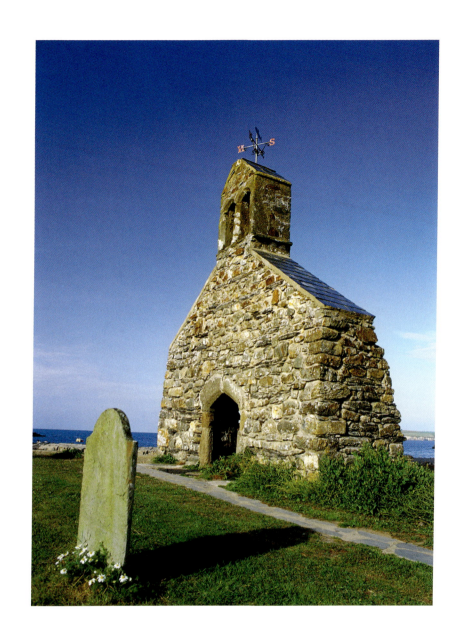

The remains of a 6th-century church, destroyed by a storm in 1839, at Cwm-yr-Eglwys, on Dinas Head, Dyfed.

The Caernarfon coast viewed from the sand dunes at Newborough Warren, on Anglesey.

The Aberdulais Falls in Neath, a favourite subject of painters in the 19th century.

A statue of Llywelyn the Great in Lancaster Square, Conwy.
Opposite: the Garreg Ddu Dam in the Elan Valley, which was flooded with four lakes in the late 19th century
to provide water for Birmingham.

The dock at Milford Haven, the huge natural harbour in southern Pembrokeshire.

The lake shore at Parc Cwm Darran, a country park near Bargoed in Mid Glamorgan.

Criccieth Castle, west of Porthmadog on the Lleyn Peninsula. It was probably built by Llywelyn the Great in the 13th century.

South Stack Lighthouse on Holy Island, off the northwest coast of Anglesey.

The chapel roof at Blaenau Ffestiniog, Gwynedd.
Opposite: looking north from Foel Cynwch on the Precipice Walk, in Snowdonia.

Carreg Cennen Castle, perched on a limestone crag in the Brecon Beacons.

Thomas Telford's suspension bridge across the Menai Strait links Anglesey to the mainland.

A ruined farmhouse near Capel Curig, a centre for walks in Gwynedd.

Betws-y-Coed, with its streams and woodland, is one of Snowdonia's most popular beauty spots.

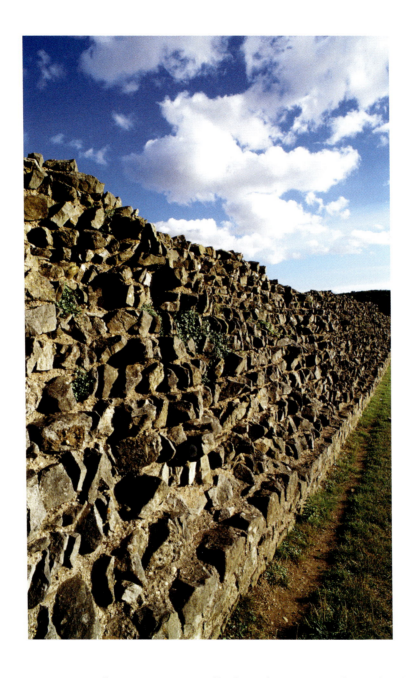

Caerwent's Roman town wall, in Gwent. Unusually, the settlement was civilian rather than military.
Opposite: Skomer Island, off the Pembrokeshire coast, is home to many rare birds.

The wonderful sands of Rhossili Beach, at the western end of the Gower Peninsula.

Penygarreg Reservoir Dam, Powys.

The Monmouth and Brecon Canal, Powys. It was built to carry coal, iron ore and limestone.

The Llangollen Railway runs along the Dee Valley from the old station in Llangollen, Clwyd.

Sgwd Isaf Clun-Gwyn (Lower White Meadow Fall) on the River Mellte in the Vale of Neath, Powys.

The ruins of Tintern Abbey, founded in 1131, lie in the Wye Valley north of Chepstow.

Strumble Head Lighthouse, west of Fishguard on the Pembrokeshire coast.
Opposite: one of the few remaining towers of the once extensive Flint Castle on the north coast.

The Pembrokeshire coast at Newgale, on St Bride's Bay, which lies on the 186-mile (298-km) coast path.

Medieval Aberconwy House in Conwy, Gwynedd, is now in the care of the National Trust.

Beaumaris Castle, Gwynedd. It was the largest of Edward I's huge fortresses built in Wales.

The River Wye flows through a steeply wooded valley at Symonds Yat, right on the Welsh border.

Anglesey, the island off the north coast of Wales, has a largely flat landscape with stone walls and houses.

The ridge of Cader Idris (the Chair of Idris), in Snowdonia National Park.

Terraced houses characterise many of the coal-mining towns in the Rhondda Valley, in Mid Glamorgan.
Opposite: Caernarfon Castle, Gwynedd. Prince Charles was invested here in 1969.

Cemaes Head on the River Teifi estuary, in Pembrokeshire.

Pen-y-Fan in the Brecon Beacons, the highest point of the national park at 2,901ft (884m).

Caerphilly Castle, in Mid Glamorgan. It covers about 30 acres (12ha) and is surrounded by a huge lake.

Carregwastad Point, a remote spot north of Fishguard in Pembrokeshire, was the landing point of French-Irish invaders in the late 18th century.

Milford Haven is now dominated by oil refineries, although it has a long history as a fishing port.

The rocky shore of Great Ormes Head, the promontory just northwest of Llandudno, in Gwynedd.

This tiny dwelling, on the quayside in Conwy, measures just 10ft (3.05m) high by 5.9ft (1.8m) wide.
Opposite: the Roman Steps, in Cwh Bychan, probably only date back to medieval times.

Garn Fawr, in the Brecon Beacons. Four mountain ranges make up the Brecon Beacons National Park.

Meolfre, a small resort on the east coast of Anglesey. Just inland is the fortified Iron Age-Romano settlement of Din Lligwy.

Pentre Ifan, a 5,000-year-old communal burial chamber near Newport in the Pembrokeshire Coast National Park. At one time the stones would have been covered by an oval-shaped mound of earth.

Castell Coch, just outside Cardiff, was built as a folly by William Burges.

Cliffs at St Bride's Bay, Pembrokeshire.

Meolfre Bay, on Anglesey. A ship, the 'Royal Charter', was wrecked off here in 1859 on its way to Liverpool from Australia. More than 450 people lost their lives.

Llangynibie bridge over the River Usk.

The Mumbles – two rocky islands off the promontory south of Swansea, in West Glamorgan.
The lighthouse dates from 1793.

Solva Harbour, at the end of a winding creek on the Pembrokeshire coast.
Opposite: the waters of Llyn Cwmorthin, between the Moelwyn and Nyth y Gigfran mountains above
Tan-y-grisiau, Gwnyedd.

Pistyll Rhaeadr, Powys. The 150-ft (46-m) falls are said to be the highest in Wales. A natural stone arch on the crags is known as the Fairy Bridge.

Lake Vyrnwy, Powys. This reservoir was built in the 1880s to supply water to Liverpool, destroying a village in the process.

Looking south across Conwy Bay to Dwygylfychi from Great Ormes Head.
Opposite: the rooftops of Llandudno, an archetypal British seaside town just below Great Orme.

Fishguard's pretty Lower Town Harbour. The town occupies the headland above.

Pistyll Rhaeadr, the highest waterfall in Wales at 240ft (73m) plunges down the sheer rockface.

The Black Mountains, a stretch of high moorland running through the Brecon Beacons National Park.

Cliffs at Holy Island, Anglesey.

Melincourt Falls, in the Vale of Neath, West Glamorgan, are part of a nature reserve.
Opposite: Conwy dock. Mussels were once an important part of the fishing industry here.

INDEX